ORANGES IN THE SNOW

You are a famous scientist, and you are working in a laboratory with your assistant Joe. You are doing an experiment on a small flower. It is a very special flower because it can help people to see in the dark.

But then somebody takes the special flower, and you can't find Joe. Is he the thief, or is it another person? What do you do next? Do you go to Joe's room, or do you look in the laboratory, or do you telephone your boss? Be careful – there is only one way to find the special flower again. But move quickly – there is not much time.

This is an interactive story. You can choose what part of the story to read next. Follow the numbers at the end of each section.

PHILLIP BURROWS AND MARK FOSTER

Oranges in the Snow

OXFORD UNIVERSITY PRESS

OXFORD
UNIVERSITY PRESS

Great Clarendon Street, Oxford OX2 6DP

Oxford University Press is a department of the University of Oxford.
It furthers the University's objective of excellence in research, scholarship,
and education by publishing worldwide in

Oxford New York

Auckland Cape Town Dar es Salaam Hong Kong Karachi
Kuala Lumpur Madrid Melbourne Mexico City Nairobi
New Delhi Shanghai Taipei Toronto

With offices in

Argentina Austria Brazil Chile Czech Republic France Greece
Guatemala Hungary Italy Japan Poland Portugal Singapore
South Korea Switzerland Thailand Turkey Ukraine Vietnam

OXFORD and OXFORD ENGLISH are registered trade marks of
Oxford University Press in the UK and in certain other countries

ISBN: 978 0 19 423429 0

Printed in Hong Kong

Word count (main text): 1710

For more information on the Oxford Bookworms Library, visit
www.oup.com/elt/bookworms

CONTENTS

Oranges in the Snow

1 The night is cold and windy. Outside the laboratory a dog howls. You are Mary Durie, the famous scientist. In your hand is a small flower. It grows in Alaska and it is very special. It can help people to see in the dark, you think.

Joe, your assistant, tells you, 'Everything's ready now. We can do the experiment.' He points to the flower.

You are a little afraid but you say, 'OK, let's start.'

■ *You begin the experiment. Go to* **18**.

2 You go to the red plane. It is full of fish. A man with a beard gets on the plane. Is he the man you want?

■ *You talk to the man on the plane. Go to 29.*

3 You telephone your boss. She is not there – she is playing tennis.

■ *Go back to* **10**.

4 You go to talk to the man. 'What are you doing here? This is private.' He runs away but he drops something. It is a ticket. 'Stop,' you say. But he runs faster.

■ *You run after the man. Go to* **12**.
■ *You look at the ticket. Go to* **20**.

5 You drink the liquid and go out of the laboratory. You can see in the dark! You walk away from the building and see a dog running after a seal. There is a man behind a car. 'What is he doing there?' you think.

■ *You telephone your boss and tell him about the flower. Go to* **22**.

■ *You go back to the laboratory and talk to Joe. Go to* **10**.

■ *You talk to the man behind the car. Go to* **4**.

6 You go to Joe's room. He is not there. You hear someone outside. 'Joe! Is that you?' Suddenly, the door closes and you can't get out.

■ *Go to* **1** *and start again.*

7 The dog drinks the liquid. After a minute, he smiles and runs away.

■ *Go back to* **18**.

8 You talk to the man with the long hair. 'We're looking for a passenger with a beard,' you say to him.

'Sorry, I can't help you. Are you looking for a watch? I have lots of watches. They are not expensive. £3? £2?'

'No, thank you. I have a watch.'

'I want a watch,' says Joe.

'We haven't time, Joe!' you say.

■ *You talk to the pilot. Go to* **30**.

9 You go to the men's table. Just then, they see you. 'Run!' says the man with the hat. 'Let's go.'

The thieves leave the restaurant fast. You and Joe run after them.

The police arrive. 'Where are they?' says a policewoman. 'It's dark and we can't see them.'

But you can see in the dark. 'They are over there,' you tell the police.

■ *Go to* **24***.*

10 You go back into the laboratory. Something is very, very wrong. There is liquid on the table and floor. The table is usually next to the window. Now it is next to the door. And where is Joe? You cannot see him. His white coat is not there – and where is the bottle?

- ■ *You go to Joe's room. Go to 6.*
- ■ *You look in this room. Go to 33.*
- ■ *You telephone your boss. Go to 3.*

11 You go up to him. 'Can we talk to you?' Joe says. 'Of course. Do you want some oranges?' the man asks. You see his face. He hasn't got a beard – but he smells of oranges.

You say, 'No. I'm sorry. You are not the right man.'

- ■ *You ask him some more questions. Go to 15.*
- ■ *You go back and follow the tracks on the right. Go to 37.*

12 You run after the man. It is not easy to run in the snow. He runs faster than you run. In front of him is a Jet-sled. 'Come back here!' you cry. 'Stop him, someone!' But the man gets on the Jet-sled – and drives away.

You walk slowly back to the laboratory. You want to talk to Joe but you cannot see him.

■ *You go back to the laboratory. Go to* **10.**

13 You follow the tracks on the left. In front of you is a delivery man. He has a box of oranges.

'Look, Joe – oranges. Is that the man?' you ask.

'I don't know,' says Joe. 'Has he got a beard?'

■ *You go up to him. Go to* **11***.*

14 There is nobody in the waiting room, but there are two more doors.

■ *You go to the shop door. Go to* **35***.*

■ *You go to the restaurant door. Go to* **23***.*

15 You ask him some more questions.

'Where do your oranges come from?' you ask.

He says, 'There is a plane at the airport. It is full of oranges from Spain.'

'Is the plane there now?' asks Joe.

'Yes – but it goes soon,' the man says.

'Are you driving back to the airport?' you ask.

'Yes. Do you want to come?'

■ *You get in his lorry. Go to **19**.*

■ *You run to the airport. Go to **27**.*

■ *You follow different tracks. Go to **34**.*

16 Joe takes the small bottle and drinks the liquid. 'Something is happening,' he says. 'I feel different. My legs and my hands hurt, but . . .' Joe goes to the window and opens the curtains. 'Mary! What's the time?'

'7 o'clock at night,' you tell him.

'It's daytime for me!' he says. Joe opens the door and looks outside.

■ *You drink the liquid too. Go to 5.*

■ *You look outside with Joe. Go to 25.*

17 You look under the table and see the dog. He is eating a shoe. 'Get out!' you say. The dog goes outside with the shoe.

■ *You look in the cupboard. Go to 31.*

18 You walk to the window. 'What are you doing?' Joe asks.

'We must be careful,' you say, and you hold up the flower. 'This is very valuable.' You look out of the window, then close the curtains. Joe locks the door.

You put the flower in a little bottle. 'OK. We are ready.'

Joe gives you a bigger bottle. It has liquid in it. You pour some liquid on the flower. It turns green. You heat the little bottle. Slowly, the liquid turns yellow. You see some red smoke. You write in your notebook, fast. Then you smile and say, 'That's it!'

■ *You give the small bottle to Joe. Go to* **16**.

■ *You drink the yellow liquid. Go to* **5**.

■ *You drop the liquid and the dog drinks it. Go to* **7**.

19 You get in his lorry. He talks a lot. He talks about his mother . . . about football . . . about his new trousers . . .

'Please,' you say. 'We must get to the airport fast.'

'Oh dear!' he says. 'I can't find my keys.'

■ *You are very slow. The thief gets away.*
  *Go to **1** and start again.*

20 You look at the ticket. It is a plane ticket to Alaska. 'Very interesting,' you think.

■ *You go back to the laboratory. Go to **10**.*

21 You go to the yellow plane. It begins to move. A minute later the plane is in the air. Is the thief on it? Perhaps he is getting away.

■ *Go to* **26**.

22 You use your mobile phone and call your boss. She says, 'Good. This can help lots of people – but don't tell anyone. Remember, there are bad men out there. Be very careful, Mary.'

■ *You go back into the building. Go to* **10**.

23 You go into the restaurant. There are lots of people there. One is wearing a white coat. Joe says, 'That's my coat!'

■ *You walk across the restaurant. Go to* **28**.

24 The police arrest the men and give the notebook, the flower and the small bottle to Joe. You and Joe can now help lots of people with the liquid.

'Why are these important?' the policewoman asks.

'Wait – and see!' you say. You look at Joe and laugh.

25 You look outside with Joe. He says, 'I can see a dog looking in the dustbins. A seal eating a fish. There's a man driving a car with no lights. This is very exciting!'

■ *You drink the liquid. Go to 5.*

26 There are only two planes left. Is the thief on the red or the blue one? You want to go to the blue plane. Joe wants to go to the red plane.

■ *You go to the blue plane. Go to 36.*

■ *You go to the red plane. Go to 2.*

27 You run to the airport and see three planes. They are all different colours – blue, yellow and red. 'Which one?' you ask Joe.

'I don't know. Can you see a man with a beard?'

'No. We haven't got much time. Let's go.'

- ■ *You go to the yellow plane. Go to **21**.*
- ■ *You go to the blue plane. Go to **36**.*
- ■ *You go to the red plane. Go to **2**.*

28 You and Joe walk across the restaurant. The man in the white coat has a beard. You can see it now. He is wearing only one shoe. The man with the beard talks to a man with a hat. 'I have it,' he says and puts a notebook on the table. You look and see it is your notebook!

The man with the hat says, 'Good! Now we can make lots of money.'

■ *You go to the men's table. Go to 9.*

29 You talk to the man. He does not want to talk to you. He says, 'Go away. I must work.'

■ *He is the thief, you think. You get the police. Go to 32.*

■ *You leave him and go to the blue plane. Go to 36.*

30 You talk to the pilot. 'I am looking for someone,' you say. 'A man with a beard who smells of oranges.'

The pilot says, 'Everyone on my plane smells of oranges. There is a man with a beard. He is in that building.' The pilot points to a building with three doors. 'Why do you want him?'

'He is a thief, I think. Can you phone the police?' you ask. Then you and Joe run to the building.

- ■ *You go in the restaurant door. Go to 23.*
- ■ *You go in the waiting room door. Go to 14.*
- ■ *You go in the shop door. Go to 35.*

31 You look in the cupboard and you find Joe. There is a scarf over his mouth and sticky tape on his hands.

'Are you OK?' you ask, and take the scarf away.

'Yes, I'm OK,' he says.

'What can you remember?' you ask.

'A man . . . with a beard. A smell of . . . oranges. A fight. His shoe in my hand . . .'

'Where is the thief?' you ask.

Joe looks at the sticky tape and says, 'The airport, perhaps?'

You go outside. 'Look!'

There are three tracks in the snow.

■ *You follow the tracks on the left. Go to* **13**.

■ *You follow the tracks on the right. Go to* **37**.

■ *You follow the tracks straight on. Go to* **34**.

32 You get the police. They ask the man lots of questions. After a long time they tell you, 'He works on the plane and he is not the man you want.' It is now very late – the thief is far away.

■ *You must begin again. Go back to* **1**.

33 You look in the room. You can't see your notebook. Or the flower. Or the small bottle with the liquid in. This is very bad. And where is Joe? Can he be a thief?

Just then you hear a noise. At first you think it is the wind.

You hear it again. It is not the wind. Where is the noise coming from?

■ *You look under the table. Go to* **17**.

■ *You look in the cupboard. Go to* **31**.

34 You follow the tracks straight on. These tracks are yours. They take you back to the building, so you follow the tracks on the right.

■ *Go to 37.*

35 You go to the shop door but the shop is closed.

■ *You go to the restaurant. Go to 23.*
■ *You go to the waiting room. Go to 14.*

36 You go to the blue plane. There are lots of boxes of oranges. A man with long hair is putting the boxes in a lorry. Next to him is the pilot. Some passengers are next to the plane, but nobody has a beard.

'Do we talk to the man with the long hair or the pilot?' you ask Joe.

■ *You talk to the pilot. Go to 30.*
■ *You talk to the man with long hair. Go to 8.*

37 These tracks go to the airport.

■ Go to **27.**

GLOSSARY

cupboard a box or space in a building; you put things in it

curtain cloth that covers a window

delivery man if you buy something, he brings it to your home or work

bread something you eat; it is made from flour

drop let fall to the ground

experiment you try an experiment to see if something works

famous you are famous if many people know you

heat when you heat something it gets hot

howl the noise an unhappy dog makes

key *(noun)* you open and lock doors with this

liquid something that isn't hard, like water

lock *(vb)* close with a key

orange fruit you eat; it grows on trees

private a place where some people are not allowed

scientist someone who finds out things about the world

smile *(vb)* you smile when you are happy

special very good or unusual

thief someone who takes something that is not theirs

valuable worth a lot of money

windy a type of weather; it makes trees and washing move

Oranges in the Snow

ACTIVITIES

Before Reading

1 **Look at the front cover of the book.**
   Are the following sentences true (T) or false (F)?

		T	F
1	The story happens in a cold place.	☐	☐
2	Someone is flying a plane.	☐	☐
3	The story is about apples on a beach.	☐	☐

2 **Look at the back cover. Complete the following sentences.**

   1 Mary Durie is a famous ……..
   2 Her laboratory is in …….
   3 She has an assistant called ……
   4 Some people steal her …..

3 **Look at the front and back covers. Guess the correct answer**
   for each question.

   1 The story is . . .
      a ☐ exciting.
      b ☐ funny.
      c ☐ a love story.
   2 The oranges are . . .
      a ☐ on the plane.
      b ☐ in the laboratory.
      c ☐ valuable.

While Reading

1 Read the first parts of the story (1 & 18).
Are these sentences true (T) or false (F)?

	T	F
1 Mary Durie holds a small flower.	☐	☐
2 Red smoke comes from the little bottle.	☐	☐
3 Joe drops some liquid on the dog.	☐	☐
4 Someone comes in the door.	☐	☐
5 A man eats the flower.	☐	☐
6 Mary Durie writes in her notebook.	☐	☐

2 Read section 31. Who does what?
Choose an answer.

1 Who is looking for Joe?
   a ☐ Mary.
   b ☐ The man with the hat.
   c ☐ The delivery man.

2 Who is in the cupboard?
   a ☐ The pilot.
   b ☐ Joe.
   c ☐ The policeman.

3 Who is wearing only one shoe?

    a ☐ The thief.

    b ☐ The dog.

    c ☐ The delivery man.

4 Who says 'Where is the thief?'

    a ☐ Mary.

    b ☐ The man with long hair.

    c ☐ The policeman.

3 **Read sections 5, 12, 18, 30, and 36. Some words are in the wrong sentences. Can you put them in the right places?**

1 The pilot points to the building at the **hat**.

2 There are boxes of oranges near the blue **airport**.

3 Mary sees a dog running after a **plane**.

4 'The man on the jet sled wears a funny **liquid**.

5 The **seal** with the long hair is putting boxes in the lorry.

6 The **man** in the little bottle turns yellow.

4 **Read sections 23, 28, 9, and 24. In this description, there are six mistakes. Which are they?**

Two men come in and sit at a table. One wears a red coat. The other one wears a funny hat. The man in the coat gives the other man a watch. Joe and Mary come into the restaurant. Mary points to the man in the coat. The two men run away. One of them wears only one glove. Mary and Joe catch them.

After Reading

1 Put these words in the right places.

*experiment   airport   sticky tape   coat   oranges   flower
restaurant   run*

Mary Durie and Joe are doing an ………… using a special
………… They make a liquid that can help people see in the
dark. A man who smells of ………… attacks Jo. The man
takes the special liquid and Joe's ………… Mary finds Jo with
………… round his hands and mouth. Joe and Mary follow
the thief to the ………… They go into a ………… and see two
men with the liquid. '…………!' shouts one of the men and
they both leave the restaurant fast. The police arrest the men
and Mary and Joe get their special liquid back.

2 In the story, what do people use these things for?

1 The sticky tape.
2 The special liquid.
3 The notebook.

3 **Answer these questions.**

1 Someone steals four things from the laboratory. What are they?

2 Where does the small flower grow?

3 Why can't the police see the thieves in the dark?

4 Why does the man with a beard smell of oranges?

5 Who phones the police?

6 Where do the tracks in the snow go?

4 **Put these sentences in the correct order.**

1 ☐ The police arrest the two men.

2 ☐ Mary drinks the liquid.

3 ☐ Someone steals the bottle.

4 ☐ The thieves are in the restaurant.

5 ☐ Mary talks to the pilot.

6 ☐ Joe is in the cupboard.

ABOUT THE AUTHORS

Mark Foster and Phillip Burrows have worked as a writer/illustrator team since 1991. They were born three years and many miles apart, but they are very nearly twins. They drive the same car, work on the same computers, and wear the same wellington boots – but not at the same time! They spend all the money they get from writing on gadgets, but please don't tell their wives. Mark and Phill have worked together on several Bookworms titles, including *Taxi of Terror* (Starter) and *Orca* (Starter). When they meet to write, they like to go to expensive hotels, eat chips dipped in coffee, and laugh at their own jokes.

OXFORD BOOKWORMS LIBRARY

Classics • Crime & Mystery • Factfiles • Fantasy & Horror
Human Interest • Playscripts • Thriller & Adventure
True Stories • World Stories

The OXFORD BOOKWORMS LIBRARY provides enjoyable reading in English, with a wide range of classic and modern fiction, non-fiction, and plays. It includes original and adapted texts in seven carefully graded language stages, which take learners from beginner to advanced level. An overview is given on the next pages.

All Stage 1 titles are available as audio recordings, as well as over eighty other titles from Starter to Stage 6. All Starters and many titles at Stages 1 to 4 are specially recommended for younger learners. Every Bookworm is illustrated, and Starters and Factfiles have full-colour illustrations.

The OXFORD BOOKWORMS LIBRARY also offers extensive support. Each book contains an introduction to the story, notes about the author, a glossary, and activities. Additional resources include tests and worksheets, and answers for these and for the activities in the books. There is advice on running a class library, using audio recordings, and the many ways of using Oxford Bookworms in reading programmes. Resource materials are available on the website <www.oup.com/elt/bookworms>.

The *Oxford Bookworms Collection* is a series for advanced learners. It consists of volumes of short stories by well-known authors, both classic and modern. Texts are not abridged or adapted in any way, but carefully selected to be accessible to the advanced student.

You can find details and a full list of titles in the *Oxford Bookworms Library Catalogue* and *Oxford English Language Teaching Catalogues*, and on the website <www.oup.com/elt/bookworms>.

THE OXFORD BOOKWORMS LIBRARY
GRADING AND SAMPLE EXTRACTS

STARTER • 250 HEADWORDS

present simple – present continuous – imperative –
can/cannot, must – *going to* (future) – simple gerunds …

Her phone is ringing – but where is it?

Sally gets out of bed and looks in her bag. No phone. She looks under the bed. No phone. Then she looks behind the door. There is her phone. Sally picks up her phone and answers it. *Sally's Phone*

STAGE 1 • 400 HEADWORDS

… past simple – coordination with *and, but, or* –
subordination with *before, after, when, because, so* …

I knew him in Persia. He was a famous builder and I worked with him there. For a time I was his friend, but not for long. When he came to Paris, I came after him – I wanted to watch him. He was a very clever, very dangerous man. *The Phantom of the Opera*

STAGE 2 • 700 HEADWORDS

… present perfect – *will* (future) – *(don't) have to, must not, could* –
comparison of adjectives – simple *if* clauses – past continuous –
tag questions – *ask/tell* + infinitive …

While I was writing these words in my diary, I decided what to do. I must try to escape. I shall try to get down the wall outside. The window is high above the ground, but I have to try. I shall take some of the gold with me – if I escape, perhaps it will be helpful later. *Dracula*

… should, may – present perfect continuous – *used to* – past perfect –
causative – relative clauses – indirect statements …

Of course, it was most important that no one should see
Colin, Mary, or Dickon entering the secret garden. So Colin
gave orders to the gardeners that they must all keep away
from that part of the garden in future. *The Secret Garden*

STAGE 4 • 1400 HEADWORDS

… past perfect continuous – passive (simple forms) –
would conditional clauses – indirect questions –
relatives with *where/when* – gerunds after prepositions/phrases …

I was glad. Now Hyde could not show his face to the world
again. If he did, every honest man in London would be proud
to report him to the police. *Dr Jekyll and Mr Hyde*

STAGE 5 • 1800 HEADWORDS

… future continuous – future perfect –
passive (modals, continuous forms) –
would have conditional clauses – modals + perfect infinitive …

If he had spoken Estella's name, I would have hit him. I was so
angry with him, and so depressed about my future, that I could
not eat the breakfast. Instead I went straight to the old house.
Great Expectations

STAGE 6 • 2500 HEADWORDS

… passive (infinitives, gerunds) – advanced modal meanings –
clauses of concession, condition

When I stepped up to the piano, I was confident. It was as if I
knew that the prodigy side of me really did exist. And when I
started to play, I was so caught up in how lovely I looked that
I didn't worry how I would sound. *The Joy Luck Club*

Mystery in London

HELEN BROOKE

Six women are dead because of the Whitechapel Killer. Now another woman lies in a London street and there is blood everywhere. She is very ill. You are the famous detective Mycroft Pound; can you catch the killer before he escapes?

The White Stones

LESTER VAUGHAN

'The people on this island don't like archaeologists,' the woman on the ferry says. You only want to study the 4,500 year-old Irish megalithic stones but very soon strange things begin to happen to you. Can you solve the mystery in time?

Escape

PHILLIP BURROWS AND MARK FOSTER

'I'm not a thief. I'm an innocent man,' shouts Brown. He is angry because he is in prison and the prison guards hate him. Then one day Brown has an idea. It is dangerous – very dangerous.

Starman

PHILLIP BURROWS AND MARK FOSTER

The empty centre of Australia. The sun is hot and there are not many people. And when Bill meets a man, alone, standing on an empty road a long way from anywhere, he is surprised and worried.

And Bill is right to be worried. Because there is something strange about the man he meets. Very strange . . .

Love or Money?

ROWENA AKINYEMI

It is Molly Clarkson's fiftieth birthday. She is having a party. She is rich, but she is having a small party – only four people. Four people, however, who all need the same thing: they need her money. She will not give them the money, so they are waiting for her to die. And there are other people who are also waiting for her to die.

But one person can't wait. And so, on her fiftieth birthday, Molly Clarkson is going to die.

Sister Love and Other Crime Stories

JOHN ESCOTT

Some sisters are good friends, some are not. Sometimes there is more hate in a family than there is love. Karin is beautiful and has lots of men friends, but she can be very unkind to her sister Marcia. Perhaps when they were small, there was love between them, but that was a long time ago.

They say that everybody has one crime in them. Perhaps they only take an umbrella that does not belong to them. Perhaps they steal from a shop, perhaps they get angry and hit someone, perhaps they kill . . .